BOOBY TRAP BOYS

Booby Trap Boys

A unique journal of the Vietnam war

David Beakey

To order additional copies of this book, contact:
Xlibris Corporation
1-888-795-4274
www.Xlibris.com
Orders@Xlibris.com
55543

CONTENTS

To Tricia Flynn,
my inspiration

1949-1967

I was born poor, in Tucson, Arizona, in 1949. My mother and father lived next to what was then called an "Indian Reservation". The Native Americans who lived there were even poorer than us. A mere generation before, their forefathers had hunted, worshiped and roamed the land freely. Occasionally, I would see one of them ride by my house on a horse, dressed in a mix of clothing; perhaps an old derby hat, a poncho, homemade pants and moccasins. My father was a WWII veteran, an anti-aircraft gunner. He fought in the Philippines and New Guinea. Of course he never spoke of his experiences in the war. But two or three times a year he would have to seek treatment for the malaria that never left his body. My father was a janitor. Another child was born. Stephen was mentally retarded and required constant attention, so my mother did not work. She stayed home and took care of the boy with Down's syndrome. We were Baptists. She never considered giving up the second son, she just accepted the fact that she would be a full time caretaker forever, until the boy died and went to heaven.

We moved to West Virginia. We lived in a trailer court. Everyone in the trailer court was poor, but they shared food and bought clothes at rummage sales. We got by. It was in West Virginia that I was introduced to the black Baptist preachers. I was amazed! They had gold teeth. They rhymed their sentences. They got sweaty and took off their jackets and threw them across the stage. They brought in singers and had choirs that sang songs like, "Troubled, Lord I'm Troubled" and "You've Got Jordan River to Cross." Sometimes, I was the only white boy in the church, but

I was always welcomed. My fathers' job title changed. Now he was a "custodian." We were still poor.

We moved to Massachusetts in 1959. We attended the First Baptist Church in Hingham. I was getting older. Our church bought us a car. We had a telephone, but could only afford a "Party Line", which meant that we shared the phone with someone in our neighborhood. I knew that my parents could never afford to send me to college. I read an article in the newspaper about Marines fighting in Vietnam. I believed in the Domino Theory. I decided to do something about my plight. My father went with me to the Marine recruitment office. I was 17 ½ years old.

Parris Island

We arrived by bus at 2:00 AM. They were waiting for us. The doors opened and I heard screaming. Lights were flashing. We stumbled out of the bus like clowns in a circus. They yelled at us, "Put your fucking shoes on those yellow painted feet, you fucking turds!" They hit us randomly. I wised up real quick. *Don't do anything out of the ordinary!, I told myself. Stay in the background. Stay invisible.*

By the time the sun came up, we had our clothes, our gear, and our new shiny heads. We were desperate clones, seeking to satisfy these three crazy men who were our Drill Instructors. They punched us and hit us with our rifles. They screamed in our faces. They taught us to march. "Platoon, Halt! Right Face! Left Face! To the Rear March! Double Time March! Use that Bayonet, you disgusting Fat Body! Let me see your War Face! Give me thirty pushups! Come on you Maggots, faster, faster! This is your rifle, this is your gun! Get your shit together ladies! You will give me 20 bends and thrusts! I got a girl named Bony Maroni! Double time it to the Rifle Range, you pieces of shit! If Chesty Puller could see you now, he'd puke! You better make this squad bay shine, girls! I can't HEAR you! Start listening to your Squad Leader. Did you check for windage, you idiot! You won't get a second chance in Viet Nam! Learn to love that M 14. Turn that knife when you pull it out of his body! Platoon 3020, you just might make it." We left Parris Island straight and tall, mean as we could be. Now we could blouse our boots and starch our hats. Advanced Infantry Training was less chaotic. Things were starting to fall into place. We learned how to fire many weapons. We threw grenades and crawled under live fire, the bullets zipping 12 inches from our bodies. We went into the gas chamber without gas masks. I liked the M 60 machine gun. I was clueless about my MOS, 0311 (Job Title). I assumed everybody was going to be a grunt. Little did I know that the machine gun would be my best friend and my worst enemy.

JUNGLE WARFARE SCHOOL

After 30 quick days of leave, I jumped on a big jet at Logan Airport, heading for a Marine Corps base I knew nothing about, other than it was in California. The Stewardesses knew where I was going; here was this skinny, ramrod straight Jarhead trying not to look worried. *Bound for Nam,* they thought. When we took off, one of them came down the long aisle, slowly, slowly . . . looking right at me! I nervously avoided her gaze. Then I saw a uniform next to me. She leaned down and whispered in my ear. "Sir, would you please come with me?" she said. I got up. Everyone was looking at us. I meekly followed her into the First Class section. There was one seat open. She said, "Wouldn't you be more comfortable here?" I gulped and sad, "Yes Ma'am, I sure would." 30 minutes later she came by to check on me. She said, "Would you like a drink?" I said, "No thanks, Ma'am." She said, "Are you sure you don't want a FREE drink? You're a Red Carpet Customer now!" "Well maybe just one." I said. When we landed in Los Angeles, they carried me off the plane. I had a big, stupid smile on my face and so did the Stewardess. I hitched a ride to the base, near Oceanside, CA.

For two months we crawled through tall grass, shot at moving targets, learned how to crack a rabbit's neck and eat it, jumped off ships to practice amphibious landings, learned what a spider hole was, fired M-16's, and practiced night ambushes. We ran night patrols. All of our Instructors were Nam vets and they were serious as Hell.

One weekend, I went down to Tijuana with three buddies. We drank, whored and rumbled all night. Just as we were heading to the US/Mexican border, nature called. I leaned up against a wall and was writing my name, when all of a sudden a carload of undercover detectives swooped down on me. Before I knew it, I was arrested, sitting in the back seat and my buddies had hightailed it back across the border. I managed a faint smile. They glared at me. They drove to the local Police Precinct. One room, one half of which was a big cell, packed with gringos. The other half was occupied by a very large, mean-looking dude, El Capitan. He had a pistola stuck in his belt. The boys started to drag me to the big cell. I didn't want to go to the big cell, thank you. They pulled harder. Suddenly, I remembered that I had taken 4 years of Spanish in High School. I looked at El Capitan. He gave me a look back. I said, "El Jefe. Por favor! Ayudame!" He said, "Porque, gringo?" I said, "Porque yo se que su pistola es el mas gran en todo el Mexico!" He burst out laughing and waived at me. "Gringo boy, sietese aqui, Hokay?" I sat next to him and made him laugh all night. In the morning he said, "Hokay, gringo boy, puede va." I said, "Adios Senor Capitan!" * I ran out the door, flagged down a cab, split the fare with a whore and jumped over the border into the states! I got back to the base camp fashionably late for roll call. One week later we boarded a plane bound for Okinawa.

---

*   Spanish translation: "Chief. Please! Help me!" "Why, American fool?" "Because I know that your pistol is the biggest in all of Mexico!" "American fool. Sit here. OK?" "OK, American fool, you can go." "Goodbye, Mr. Captain!"

DA NANG (JANUARY, 1968)

Our plane landed noisily on the corrugated steel runway. We were told to run off the aircraft and form a perimeter. Rockets were falling out of the sky. The heat blasted our faces. After a few minutes there was an all clear siren. We hustled to our assigned barracks. After we were given weapons, we were told to mount up on waiting trucks. We were part of a convoy, headed north. We traveled through Phu Bai, Hue, Quang Tri and Dong Ha on our way to the firebase at Con Thien. Suddenly the shit hit the fan! The TET Offensive had begun. There were explosions everywhere. Our convoy was ordered back to Hue City. We stopped on the outskirts and were ordered to help a company sized patrol that was sweeping a village. Help? We were so green that we barely remembered to put our magazines into our M-16's! But we learned quickly. I just followed orders and ended up entering a hooch, where a family lived. It was empty. Suddenly, I spotted a basket that moved. From underneath came a face. I raised my rifle. Something told me not to shoot. I finally realized that it was a civilian woman, shaking with fear. She gave me a look. I looked at her and tried to smile. My face was frozen. I backed out of the hooch and continued looking for bad guys. Two of my friends were wounded that day. Later we arrived at Con Thien. It was a huge hill, with heavily fortified bunkers and a deep trench line that ran around the perimeter. We ran from the trucks up the hill to the Command Post. Deep inside the Command Post, by the light of candles, we met Lieutenant Young. The first thing he said was, "I need three volunteers to be machine gunners." There were five of us sitting there. FNG's (fucking new guys). I slowly raised my hand. Two marines reluctantly followed my lead. My fate was sealed.

PATROL

"I don't mind chopping wood and I don't care if the money's no good
Take what you need and leave the rest
They should never have taken the very best."
                                    Robbie Robertson

We headed into the jungle. The mission was to search out and engage the enemy. Little did we know that we were to become the hunted. Things deteriorated quickly. The monsoon had been threatening for a week, with scattered but intense rain and on the first day of the weeklong patrol the skies opened up. Sheets of rain fell, quickly filling the rice paddies. We were forced to walk on dikes and raised trails, against our better judgment. This made our progress more predictable and we were higher off the ground, silhouetted as we walked. Nevertheless, we trudged along, grimly seeking contact. At night we huddled in a large circle, in foxholes filled with water. We wrapped ponchos around ourselves and put the cellophane wrappings from our C Ration cigarette packages over the barrels of our weapons. Those on watch peered into the darkness, secretly praying that we wouldn't be assaulted at night. At dawn, we saddled up and continued the hunt. On the third day we lost our first man. A single sniper round went through his pack and lodged in his shoulder. He was taken away by chopper in the afternoon. He got that million dollar wound. We knew he was on his way to the hospital ship and then maybe on to Japan. Later the point man nearly tripped an artillery round, rigged across the trail. It was a fresh booby trap, and we looked at the jungle around us, which was quiet except for the hiss of the constant rain. On day four a grenade was tossed into a group of three men who had huddled together to eat. Two managed to scramble away, but one man was frozen in place and was wounded. The corpsman gave him a shot of morphine to still his screams. By now, we secretly wished we could throw away the extra machine gun ammo that we carried, into the three feet of water we trudged through. Our feet were bleeding and swollen from the constant submersion. The rain had only gotten heavier, continuing through the night.

On day six there was a short burst of automatic gunfire at the head of the column. One man was wounded immediately. We opened up, shooting in every direction, into clumps of trees and in the general direction of the hostile fire. But the enemy had quickly withdrawn, leaving nothing but a few bullet casings and bent branches. Again a chopper came, for the third time. That night, we heard strange noises through the rainfall, a mournful wailing in the distance. Some thought it was a Vietnamese song, being broadcast over a transistor radio. Others thought it was the voice of spirits, drifting through the jungle. In the morning, a small Viet Cong flag hung from a tree, only meters from our position.

By now, we were weary and agitated. We no longer walked stealthily, but stomped through the sodden trails, barely looking to the right or left. At noon we received more sniper fire. There were no injuries; the rounds flew high over our heads, seeming to be more of a statement than a threat. We trudged on, through the rain.

At dusk, we finally rendezvoused with the choppers, which were to carry us home, to the base camp. As we were boarding, there was more hostile fire, some rounds slamming against the sides of the choppers. The door gunners let loose with abandon, but only a few of us fired, preferring instead to ensure a spot on the choppers, the birds of freedom. As we rose above the jungle, we stared sullenly, thinking only of changing our stinking clothes and getting dry. Below us, in the jungle, other men looked up at the choppers. They too were glad that the mission had ended. They turned and crept away, thinking of the warmth of their tunnels.

Body Snatch

It was bad. We got caught in a perfectly executed ambush. Sometimes I can't help but be amazed by the talent of our enemy. They cut us up. And amid the shouting, the firing and the mass confusion, we left one man behind. A comrade who was killed as soon as the shooting started. As we retreated, we could see his body, but there was a field of fire that was so intense it prevented us from approaching.

Today, our mission is to retrieve that body. We are honor bound to bring him back. At the same time, everyone knows that this is a set up. The site where he fell is an excellent place for us to be hit again. We suspect that the body itself may be booby trapped. The enemy is still active in the area and we know that they'll be waiting for us, watching as we come back, knowing that we must return. But not one man considers any alternatives. We will go and there is no discussion, other than how best to accomplish this task. We've all been on these missions before, "body snatches". And some of us have seen things go very badly. Once we lost a man while retrieving a body. So we use our experience and make a plan. We will first run a feint, send a team in to draw fire and then follow up with another team from a different direction. Then we will get close enough so that two men (volunteers) can throw long lines with hooks attached toward the body. We will then drag the body to us and under covering fire, if necessary, bring him back to the safety of our position. Then the chopper will come and he will be on his way home to the States, to his mother.

We are saddled up now, heavy with firepower and the extra equipment. Each man is alone with his thoughts as we leave the fire base. Secretly, we thank God that it is not us that our fellow marines are going to retrieve. Then we enter the jungle and we think only of the mission.

Dog Day Afternoon

They were stretched out underneath a tree, side by side. The dog handler and his dog. What a team! My squad had never worked with them before, but they sure delivered. They led us right to the enemy. We had to run to keep up. After a brief firefight, I looked around for them. Then I heard the news. They had both been shot. It didn't surprise me. They had been too far ahead of us and had not only found the enemy, but had become the first casualties as well. And now they were lying there in the partial shade, waiting to be airlifted out of the jungle. There were a total of 4 wounded (including the dog). The chopper appeared as if out of nowhere, *deus ex machina*, settling down to gather up our wounded and whisk them off to the land of sheets and nurses. We put two men into the chopper. The Co Pilot held up one finger, meaning he could take one more casualty. Two marines went over to the dog handler and started to lift him up. He started shouting and pointing to the dog. Finally, they understood. He wanted the dog taken out before him. The marines lifted the dog up and carried him to the chopper. When a second chopper arrived, the dog handler was placed aboard. As his chopper ascended, I couldn't shake the image of the two of them. They were so tight! They had formed a bond so strong that it transcended comradeship and rested at a level so deep only they could understand it.

A Rifle: Dropped Once, Never Fired

W e were running night patrols with the ARVN's. You had to give them credit for one thing; they were practical. One day, a few of them were swimming off the shore of the island we temporarily inhabited. Suddenly, one of them disappeared. He slid beneath the surface. His friends started yelling and there was a lot of confusion. Then, they located him. He had been underwater for about three minutes. He looked dead to me. Kind of gray and motionless. Two of them grabbed him by the ankles and they held him upside down. They shook him and water poured out of his mouth. He made a few noises and they laid him down. He finally sat up with a strange, embarrassed look on his face. He smiled and all of his friends laughed. Soon they were swimming again.

Later that day, their sergeant was discussing the details of our night patrol. The marine sergeant said, "We go on patrol at 2200 hours." The ARVN sergeant said, "No, No! We go at 2000 hours!" The marine sergeant asked him why the time mattered. The ARVN sergeant said, "2200 hours, VC come out!" Like I said, they were practical.

THE JOKE

We rested on the side of the hill. Two marines, tired and exhilarated from the recent skirmish. We took long drinks of water from our canteens and shared a joint, recounting the events of the day. Most of those details were boring; the preparation, the journey and the waiting, so we concentrated on the short period of mayhem, the main event. "Man, I was pinned down for half an hour!" "Did you see that Phantom jet swoop down on them? He was so low I could see his face!" "I threw all my grenades in the first five minutes!"

Next to us, almost totally covered by a poncho, lay a fellow marine. Only his boots stuck out, his feet crossed. The sun beat down on him. Perhaps he was sleeping. Occasionally, we would steal glances at him. We did not know him. This was a large operation, he could be anyone. We continued to talk, still full of energy. Finally, I looked again at the prone marine. "Man, he's sleeping like a log!" "Yeah, it's amazing how he doesn't move," replied my buddy. We both laughed but quickly looked away. We chatted for several more minutes, oblivious to our comrade and everyone else around us. Choppers were coming and going, stirring up dust at the top of the hill. All of the wounded and killed had been taken away. We finished the joint. The sun beat down on us.

Glancing at the marine next to us my buddy said, "Man, I guess that guy is dead tired!" We exploded into laughter. But we soon stopped laughing and again looked away. After resting we started to get our gear together. It was time to rejoin our unit and start preparing positions for the night.

From above, the chopper pilot saw the two of us. As he was looking away, his gaze was drawn to their comrade, lying next to them. He swore under his breath. He turned to the copilot and said, "I just spotted a KIA that no one informed us about. We'll have to go back down and get him."

As the chopper made its turn, we were already moving up the hill, carrying our rifles casually. I turned and looked at the fallen marine. I grinned and shook my head. My grin slowly turned into a tight line. My eyes were dead.

BLINDED BY THE LIGHT

We set up our night perimeter. A large circle on the top of a huge sand dune. 100 yards away, the jungle surrounded us. Just after dusk we were crouched down, talking softly. I was the team leader and the machine gunner. As usual, we were short a man. We also had an assistant machine gunner and an ammo humper. We talked about the usual topics; what we would do when we rotated back to the states, who was going to stand watch first, who wanted to trade cigarettes for C Rations.

Suddenly, _____ decided to light up a smoke. Of course he told no one. He cupped the cigarette in his two hands. I saw a flicker of light and was just about to yell at him when all Hell broke loose. A VC opened up from the tree line with an automatic burst of fire. I fell over and rolled instinctively. Sand kicked up into my eyes. I couldn't see a thing. I thought that I'd been shot in the eyes. I felt a rush of panic in my chest. I forced myself to calm down. I took a few deep breaths. I rubbed my eyes and slowly my vision returned. I shook my head. The entire episode took about two minutes. I rolled over again, this time toward the machine gun. I put my finger on the trigger and let loose with one long burst of fire at the spot where I had seen a flash of light, just before I "was hit". My gun went, "Bam, bam, bam, bam, bam, bam, bam!" The tracers helped me guide my fire, but of course gave away our position. I stopped firing. Everything was quiet for awhile, then marines started shouting. I had really gotten everyone's attention.

A few minutes later it became quiet again. I gave _____ a look. Then the Sergeant crawled over to our position. He wasn't happy. "Great job, Beakey! Now you've got to move your whole gun team to a new position." I kept quiet about the cigarette. After we moved to our new position things settled down. Life in the bush continued. Monotony followed by moments of terror.

THE PRISONER

It was the picture of the Playmate of the Year that confused us. We found it inside his leather wallet, carefully folded. We were going through the prisoner's belongings, most of which were predictable; food, ammunition, field dressings and such. But then there was the picture, cut out from a French magazine and tucked away. It befuddled us. Why would a Viet Cong carry such a thing? We discussed it. We argued about it. Some of us had trouble putting the two things together, The Playmate and our enemy, a Viet Cong. It was much easier to envision him as a beast, a gook, or as a larger than life, evil thing, a King Kong, for example. But this discovery, the picture, was disturbing. Some us thought of home, "the world", where events were occurring at a rapid pace, perhaps passing us by. We had heard rumors of hippies marching on Washington, "Be Ins" and "Love Ins". It made our heads hurt, and we felt out of touch. We tried to stay current, stay hip. We listened to Hendrix and the Beatles when possible, on small transistor radios, pressed against our ears as we hunkered in our foxholes. But we knew that we were getting a sanitized version, via the Armed Forces Radio. Now we wondered, as we rummaged through the bare belongings of one of our enemy, "Can this guy, who lives in tunnels and eats nothing but rice, be more hip than us?"

We passed the picture around, handling it as if it were part of the Dead Sea Scrolls. Then we gazed at the prisoner. He squatted impassively, behind the barbed wire. He was small and young. He wore nothing but black shorts. His eyes burned with passion, but he did not meet our gaze. He looked beyond us. He no longer bothered with war. His thoughts were now solely of the woman, the woman in the picture, the woman with frosted hair and perfect skin.

THE FRAGGING

W e were in the bush, on a two or three day operation. We were running daytime patrols, then moving on, setting up a platoon-sized perimeter at dusk, and then, of course, moving the whole perimeter several hundred yards when it became dark. We did this because we knew we were being watched at all times. This night we set up around an abandoned village. Most of the huts had been destroyed and there wasn't much left of the village, just holes and mounds of dirt which we improvised for defensive purposes. Of course the grunts were on the actual perimeter. The Lieutenant, Sergeant Gordon the radioman and the corpsman set up the command post in our center. They were inside the only structure remaining, a hooch made out of some type of clay or cement. It had four walls and an opening that was formerly a door. It had no roof.

We settled in for the evening, one grunt from each fire team standing watch, which meant laying down, facing out, watching and listening for activity. After three hours, he would wake up another member of the fire team, for his turn. At about 0100 I heard a grenade explode, close enough so that I thought that we were being attacked. Within two minutes, another grenade exploded. I heard men running and my throat went dry, my chest went ice cold, as I thought we were being overrun. Then it was quiet. We were all up, rifles in our hands, trying to figure everything out. Then there was a commotion from the CP. I was a squad leader at the time. I went to the CP. I could smell the smoke from the grenades. There were several other marines standing around, so it started to become clear to me that we hadn't been attacked. We gave each other looks.

Inside the CP, three men had been slightly wounded; the radioman, the corpsman and Sergeant Gordon. I realized that someone had fragged them. I knew at once who the target was: Sergeant Gordon He was a by-the-book marine. This was his second tour. A lot of the men didn't like him because he was not tolerant of certain things. He disapproved of those of us who smoked pot, even though we never did it in the bush, only at firebases, when we were technically "off duty." He was a "John Wayne" type who never goofed around, was always in battle-mode and didn't like complainers. I really wasn't fond of him, but secretly respected him.

None of the men were badly wounded. They had small shrapnel wounds. Surprisingly enough, after about an hour, we all went back to our positions and those not on watch went to sleep. I don't know exactly what was decided later at the CP that night, but in the morning, we ate and moved out. Nothing officially was ever said. Of course there were rumors about who did it, but there was no proof. About a month later, we were out on patrol and Sergeant Gordon was wounded by enemy fire. He had a leg wound. We were on our way back to a base camp when it happened. We were about 1000-2000 yards from the base camp. Two marines started to carry Sergeant Gordon to the base camp. He wouldn't hear of it. He insisted on hobbling in under his own power. Some of the men mumbled that he was showing off, others whispered that they were glad he got hit. Several of us were quiet and said nothing. I remember thinking somehow, he knew something that I didn't know, that he wasn't so bad after all.

I sometimes hear old marines talking about fragging, and how it is "just part of war." I'm not so sure about that. I think if you hate a man enough to kill him, there are other ways to go about it.

Sky Pilot

"In the morning they return
With tears in their eyes
The stench of death drifts up to the skies
A soldier so ill looks at the sky pilot
Remembers the words
"Thou shalt not kill."
Sky pilot,
Sky pilot,
How high can you fly?
You'll never, never, never reach the sky."

Eric Burden

Preparing for the service he paused as he picked up the flak jacket. He put it on and shook his head, smiling slightly. *If only my wife could see me now*, he thought. Next came the helmet, somewhat ill fitting. Unlike us, he had not written anything on his helmet, not even the town of his origin, Bakersfield, California. Finally, he faced his biggest decision; whether to tuck the 45 inside his flak jacket. He looked outside his bunker, at the hills surrounding the base camp. He noticed how close the tree line was to the trenches. He remembered the sniper fire and constant incoming rounds that had kept us on edge recently. And he thought of the probes, now nightly, when the claymores had been turned around and the razor wire cut. He decided to compromise. He picked up the weapon, but didn't chamber a round. As he left the bunker, he tucked his well-worn bible under his arm.

He walked toward us. We waited impatiently for his words of wisdom and comfort. He marveled at how such young men could look so weary. Suddenly, he felt nervous, unsure of himself. He knew that we were going on patrol later, at dusk. Would we all return? He considered changing his prepared sermon, but of what should he speak? Safety? Forgiveness? Trust? We stirred slightly, sensing his doubt. He felt panic rising in his throat. He had spent three months with us and was no longer naïve, or so he thought. He knew we were going hunting later. Should he wish us good luck? His sermon remained tucked inside his pocket. He decided to pray. Silently, he asked the Lord to guide him. At once he felt better. Still ignoring his prepared sermon, he let his bible fall open. His eyes fell on Psalm 31.

He started to read: "In thee, O Lord, do I put my trust; let me never be ashamed: deliver me in my righteousness. Bow down thine ear to me; deliver me speedily: be thou my strong rock, for an house of defence to save me. For thou art my rock and my fortress; therefore for thy name's sake lead me, and guide me. Pull me out of the net that they have laid privily for me: for thou art my strength. Into thine hand I commit my spirit: thou hast redeemed me, O Lord God of truth." When he finished, he looked at us. We gazed back at him with skeptical eyes. He felt powerful, through the Word.

And then it was dusk. He walked slowly to his bunker, nestled in the center of the base camp. He often wondered what it was like living in the trenches and small bunkers that ringed the perimeter. He knew that even if a large force attacked the base at night, no enemy would make it as far as his bunker, that the first line of defenders would hold. This feeling of security, tainted by the knowledge that others might die so that he would live, stayed with him until sleep gradually carried him away. While he slept, red flares lit up the night sky. We had found the action we both hoped for and dreaded.

And then it was dawn. He heard the news soon after awakening . . . two marines dead, blown away, another wounded. Three VC killed, 2 AK 47's and documents retrieved from the skirmish area. He raced down to meet us as we walked back into the base camp. We were haggard and grim. He tried to think of words that would welcome us home and convince us that the tradeoff had been worth it. He suddenly realized that in his haste he had left his bible in his bunker. His throat felt dry and for a brief moment he was dizzy. We were drawing closer. Our point man advanced towards him . . .

ASCENSION

We arose at dawn. There was excitement in the air. One hundred men were preparing to fly away, into the brightening skies, and descend into sure trouble. The Captain had briefed the platoon leaders. They in turn had passed on word to the squad leaders, who filtered the facts down to the rest of us. It was like planning a surprise party for yourself. We knew that the choppers would come and whisk us away. We also knew that, as in the case of most surprise parties, the cat was out of the bag. Our visit to the badlands was expected by those we were to engage. This thought made my stomach go cold, so I decided to stretch my legs. As I walked by small groups of men, I noticed how they prepared for our departure. Some cooked an elaborate breakfast, piling three heat tabs together and spreading out several C Ration cans, preparing a three course meal. Others wrote final messages that they secreted in various areas; their helmet liner, inside their flak jacket, in their boot. *Dear Mom, if you get this letter . . .* Others laughed and joked too loudly. Most fiddled with their gear, making last minute adjustments. What seemed like enough ammo a few minutes ago was now deemed insufficient. There was always room for a few more grenades. Some of the new guys were pale and quiet. They stood out today, and many of us were already avoiding them, not wanting to be near their clumsy terror.

Suddenly a few of us, then others, heard that unmistakable sound. Choppers in the distance. I had an urge to get sick, but stifled it. The noise got louder as we stood up and started to form small, pre-organized boarding groups. Simultaneously, packs were hoisted, helmets fell, loose machine gun rounds rattled against gear, radios squawked, officers yelled and the thumping of the chopper blades filled the air. A few marines had forgotten to chamber a round and now their bolts clicked home. My throat was dry and adrenaline pumped through my body. Our chopper landed and I started to run toward it, feeling light and happy. We scrambled aboard, saying nothing, but sharing that fear and excitement that only warriors know. Soon, we were airborne, partygoers bearing gifts of battle.

The Man Who Fell
From The Sky

---

*"We're coming out with our dead, our wounded and our equipment.
We're coming out as Marines."*
Marine General, Korean War, 1951

He was heavy in a cumbersome way. We carried him quietly, emitting only soft grunts as we worked our way down the mountain. We also carried full packs, our weapons and extra ammo. We wore flak jackets and helmets. Sweat trickled down our faces as we tried to keep up with the rest of our unit. The fighting was over, at least for the time being.

Earlier in the day, we had climbed the mountain, to rendezvous with the choppers and be carried away, back to Hill 881. But things went terribly wrong. The enemy let us approach the summit, even allowed us to set up a perimeter in the high grass. The trees formed a dense canopy and it was difficult to find a good landing zone for the choppers, which were to swoop in and pick us up quickly, barely setting down. This area was considered "hot". We were part of a force that was securing the hills, one by one. It was slow going and we were taking casualties, because the enemy was well established and not afraid to engage us in short but fierce battles. Some hills had to be retaken, often two or three times. This particular hill was highly dangerous, as it was covered with trees and dense foliage, not bare like most of the others. I didn't like this hill and I was eager to jump on the chopper and be whisked away. As we waited for the unmistakable sound of the ride home, it seemed eerily quiet. Suddenly one, then all of the men heard the choppers. Eventually they appeared, first one then others, circling the top of the hill. Someone tossed a smoke grenade and quickly, the lead chopper moved in to pick up the first squad. I peered up, through the trees and saw the second chopper and a third, hovering just above the treetops. I could tell that the pilots were impatient and wanted to get in and out as quickly as possible. I ran toward the first chopper, my eyes fixed on it as it descended. I could see the door gunner, poised to fire, if necessary. Suddenly the chopper disappeared in a flash of light. I shook my head and looked again. There was nothing there. Then, another explosion, high in the trees. I turned and watched as the second chopper dipped crazily and plummeted to earth. Another explosion rocked the ground beneath me, and I finally realized that it was a helicopter ambush.

They were firing RPG's at the choppers. We scrambled for cover. Smoke filled the air. We formed a defensive position and fired into the trees surrounding us. It gradually became quieter until the only noise was the sound of the surviving chopper gunning its engines as it quickly regained altitude and flew away. The sound grew fainter and fainter. Soon, we were alone again. After settling down, we surveyed the scene. Only two men on the ground were wounded. The choppers and their crews had not been so lucky. Two choppers were destroyed, blown apart. All crewmembers had perished. The bodies were scattered like rag dolls among machinery and pieces of metal. I walked among the wreckage. It seemed surreal. Soon, the Captain decided that we would walk back down the hill and hump three kilometers, to a small base camp. If we left immediately, we would make it by sunset. There was no discussion regarding the bodies. We would carry them out.

I tried not to look at his face. But I couldn't help seeing his hair. The pilot had bright red hair. And he was tall, well over six feet. His flight suit seemed out of place. I was used to the jungle fatigues that we wore. The flight suit reminded me of a space suit. All the grunts respected the men who came from the sky, to pull out the wounded or drop supplies, or get them out of tight spots. Now I carried the man carefully and made a silent promise not to drop him, to be respectful. But I never looked at his face. And when we got to the base camp and our job was done, I laid down and gazed at the stars, unable to sleep, unable to admit that the man from the sky was just like me.

Cleo's Bad Day

"She tells him she thinks she needs to be free. He tells her he doesn't understand. She takes his hand. She tells him nothing's working out the way they planned. She's so many women. He can't find the one who was his friend."

Warren Zevon

The day Cleo got his Dear John letter we were on a hill overlooking Khe Sanh. This was the third time we had taken this hill. Every time we left, a spotter plane or a recon unit would let us know that they had seen NVA on the hill again. It became like a game. We just wanted the hill to be unoccupied and they wanted to use the hill to call in artillery strikes on the airstrip and ammo dump at Khe Sanh. It always seemed unfair to me that we had all kinds of air power and they didn't have any, south of the DMZ. But they had their advantages too; they knew the land, they were supplied with modern weapons by Russia and China, and they had years of experience fighting a guerrilla war. Some of the bunkers they constructed on the hill we now occupied could take a direct hit from anything short of a B 52 and sustain little damage.

A chopper dropped some C Rations, ammo and mail. We hadn't received mail in three weeks. Everyone gathered around as the Gunny yelled out our names. Most of us got at least one letter. I found a quiet place and was reading my letter when I heard an ungodly wailing sound from the other side of the hill. I went over to check it out. Cleo was standing with a crumpled letter in his hand. We all respected Cleo. He came from Chicago and was a member of the Blackstone Rangers. He got shot *before* he arrived in Nam. He was usually a cool customer, and had a regal way about him, even under fire. Doc (he wasn't a Corpsman, we just called him Doc) was Cleo's best friend. He went up to Cleo and took the letter out of his hand. Sure enough, it was the classic Dear John letter. "You've been gone so long . . .", "Your friend Duck has been coming around . . .", "I was just so lonely . . ." We all dreaded getting a letter like that, a letter that makes it clear that Jody has taken over. We didn't know what to say.

Cleo picked up his M 16 and walked away from us. I was frozen. Should I run after him, shouldn't somebody do something? We all expected to hear a shot, but it was quiet. We milled around feeling awkward. Doc started walking in the direction Cleo had gone. Eventually, most of us went back to our positions. We gave each other looks, but that was about it. About two hours later I saw Cleo. He was talking with two of his friends, members of his squad. I saw him say something and the other two marines started laughing. Even Cleo managed a faint smile. After he got that letter, he didn't seem to change at all. One time, about a month later, we were at a base camp and I was smoking a joint with him. I mentioned something that was bothering me. He looked at me and said, "It ain't nothing but a thing." You know, he was right.

TWO GENERALS

I bumped into two generals at Khe Sanh. Since I was there for only two months, that might seem strange. But looking at the bigger picture, it makes more sense. Khe Sanh was big news. All of America had heard of the assault by NVA troops and the terrific defense mounted by the 26th marines. Our group, 2/1, and others, relieved the 26th in April,1968. We humped through the bush, parallel to Route 9 in the mountains, during Operation Pegasus.

My first encounter with a general was somewhat awkward. I needed to get from one side of the perimeter to the other, and decided to go straight across the airstrip. The airstrip was a mess, and included huge chunks of metal, gouged out by mortars and artillery rounds. There was a dead C130, next to a hole. The hole was a half-hearted attempt to "bury" the plane, but incoming rounds had put an end to that. Even in May, planes couldn't land, due to the poor shape of the airstrip and the number of artillery rounds that rained in on the base. Most marines avoided the airstrip, as it was like a huge football field; totally bare and open. But I was in a hurry, so I set out and hoped for the best.

Once I started hustling, I had tunnel vision. I was focused on the far trench line. Soon, though, I noticed a lone figure striding towards me. I knew instinctively that he was an officer. As we neared each other, I knew, somehow, that he was a high ranking officer. Soon, I got close enough to realize that he was a general. We walked directly towards each other, the only humans on top of Khe Sanh, on the "strip". I knew that he was worried that I would panic and salute him. We came face to face. I cleared my throat and said, "Afternoon Sir". He said, "Afternoon, marine." He gave me a look. We then went about our business.

The second time I saw a general at Khe Sanh, it was not so pleasant, not so mundane. I was walking near the airstrip. By now, choppers were landing regularly. The choppers were delivering supplies, but also stopping by to disembark combat troops, sometimes directly from firefights. Once I saw a tall black marine run off a chopper. His eyes were wide and he was waving a 45 pistol. On another day, I saw 3 combat news photographers lined up neatly, on the ground. They had been killed in an ambush, on Route 9. I was ashamed when some marines stole their cameras, as they lay there, quiet and dead.

I was up by the airstrip again the next day. A company had spent several days flushing out some NVA mortar positions and snipers. A chopper landed and I helped unload some dead marines. They were put in body bags and laid out on the red dirt. There were 6 body bags. Then I noticed a general, nearby. He walked over to the bags, as another chopper hovered nearby. He bent over and partially unzipped a bag. I could see the marine's face, gray, with his eyes half-open. The general paused. He shook his head. His lips came together and for a moment, his sorrow was evident. He didn't think anyone was watching. He zipped up the bag and turned away. I know the generals and other top officers are always willing to sacrifice a certain amount of troops to attain their goals. But I never thought that they were human beings. My brief glimpse that day helped me see things from their point of view. They had feelings. But I still think that generals need to see a lot more things from *our* point of view.

THE NEW LIEUTENANT

He arrived at Khe Sanh raring to go. Of course he had a 4 year college degree and Officer Training School under his belt, but he looked pretty young. We distrusted all the 2nd Lieutenants. They were green, just out of Quantico, and they wanted to lead marines, kill the enemy and make rank. Hardly any of them were smart enough to listen to the Gunnery Sergeants and the Staff Sergeants, who had years of experience and of course they never asked us for advice. We had relieved the 26th Marines, who had withstood the siege at Khe Sanh. We cleared the mountains and Route 9 on Operation Pegasus and now we took over the base camp while those brave men went somewhere else, hopefully to recover from the unsuccessful siege. The NVA had dug trenches to within 50 meters of the barbed wire. They had fired artillery shells from as close as Hill 881 and as far away as Laos. They had probed the perimeter nightly. But they couldn't overrun Khe Sanh as they had Dien Bien Phu. We were still taking a lot of artillery rounds daily, some sniper fire, and it was still so hot that the C 130's wouldn't land on the airstrip which was pockmarked with holes from exploding bombs. There were also some wrecked planes on the airstrip, left there where they had been shot to pieces. So they dropped supplies to us by helicopter.

The Lieutenant had been at Khe Sanh about one week. We were saddling up to go out on patrol. Our mission was to investigate enemy activity about 1 ½ kilometers from the base camp at a bunker compound that the NVA had constructed during the original siege. We walked out of the base camp cautiously, there were land mines everywhere. We neared the area where some recon marines had seen NVA in the old bunkers. The Lieutenant was eager to catch and kill some bad guys. He kept walking further and further in front of us. He thought he was John Wayne. He yelled, "Come on men, assault the position!" He was far ahead of us now. We lost sight of him. There were some NVA in the area. We had a brief firefight and then they fled. We looked around for the new Lieutenant. He was nowhere to be seen. We started a thorough search. Eventually we found him. He was in a bunker, dead. His weapon, gear, boots and most of his clothes were gone. He had advanced so far ahead of us, his adrenaline pumping, his mind full of theoretical training, that they had just snatched him and killed him quickly. I never even learned his name.

The Close Call

We left the safety of the fire base. Our task was to set up a night ambush. We set in amongst a group of haggard trees and sharp bushes. The sun set as we tried to ward off the insects and rough foliage. Once it became fully dark, we moved again, 200 meters away, into the sand dunes. The wind whistled quietly and the scattered clumps of grass fluttered slightly. The sand dunes supplied ready-made foxholes; slight depressions in the ground. We were grateful, but didn't want to be so low that we couldn't scan the horizon. Now it was my turn. I rolled over and shook my head at 0400. My job was to be alert and observant until 0600, at which time we would head back to the fire base. At about 0500, as dawn was slowly creeping across the sky, I saw some movement. I tried to focus on the apparitions before me. Slowly, they came into focus; at least 6 figures, in uniform, crouched and running parallel to our position. I could see their weapons. I aimed my rifle at the 1st soldier. Then I hesitated and considered putting my rifle on automatic. I could rake across the group and hope to hit three or four of them. I sighted down the rifle. The sun was peeking over the dunes. The mist was slowly evaporating. I had a great bead on him. I started to squeeze the trigger. Suddenly, I had doubts. The men were running awkwardly. They resembled Americans. I eased off the trigger. I watched them for about 60 seconds and realized they were marines, probably from our platoon. Yes, they were lost and trying to find us. We were never notified that two squads were going out this night. I whistled, and their heads turned. They were startled and then happy that they had encountered "friendlies" instead of bad guys. Our squad had hoped to find bad guys that night. We walked back to the outpost together. One squad was disappointed, the other squad grateful.

GARWOOD

In 1965, PFC Garwood was captured by VC soldiers south of Da Nang. He spent 14 years in captivity. Many people, including US POWs who spent time with him in the tiger cages and temporary camps of the VC, accused him of collaborating with the enemy. He learned to speak fluent Vietnamese, translated orders between the captors and captives, was given special attention, and later, after being handed over to the NVA, even walked point for them with an AK 47 slung around his neck.

Garwood was brought up on charges when he returned to America. He was given a Dishonorable Discharge from the Marine Corps. Some thought he should have been shot by a firing squad. Others weren't so sure. They wondered how they would have coped, under similar circumstances. Almost all of Garwood's fellow POW's during the first 5 years, died in captivity. Subsequent studies, based on the famous "Stockholm Syndrome" and the experience of Patty Hearst have indicated that certain people are more easily converted while in captivity. They relinquish their will in order to survive. But others, such as John McCain, never give in.

Garwood swears that his AK 47 was never loaded, a claim that has some credibility, due to the fact that the NVA did force captives to walk point, unarmed, much as human shields. I give him a lot of credit. That man knew how to stay alive.

Thanksgiving 1968

The rumor was getting stronger by the hour. We were to receive a hot turkey dinner today. All we had to do was run a typical patrol and then the choppers would meet us near the China Sea with a Thanksgiving meal. This was too good to be true! We prepared for our patrol with a little more enthusiasm than usual, as could be expected. Our minds were on that turkey. During the briefing we only half listened. We were to leave the fire base, sweep through the leper colony looking for weapons and tunnels, and then rendezvous with the choppers at the sand dunes. We had done this before. The leper colony was considered a hostile village. We usually took sniper fire from it and the outlying rice paddies were loaded with booby traps. But we had an uneasy agreement with the villagers, so there was never a pitched battle. They cooperated with us in a minimal fashion and we never mistreated them. Each of us knew the sentiments of the other, and we each looked for the edge, on a daily basis. Occasionally, one side or the other lost people in the vicinity of that village, but when we entered it, they acquiesced to our firepower and behaved themselves. We all knew the drill. So as the Lieutenant explained our objective, our minds were drifting, thinking about that meal. We left at 1400 hours. We were on the outskirts of the village within half an hour. Everything was routine. A few women were working in the fields. Some children wandered towards us, keeping a safe distance, but hoping for handouts if we stopped to rest. Two old men walked along the path as we advanced. We entered the village.

As usual, all eyes were on us, but the villagers feigned nonchalance. We were getting hungry. We checked out several huts and looked for any suspicious signs, anything that might indicate hiding places or unusual activity. It was the same old leper colony. We never were too comfortable here and were always happy to leave. Soon the lead elements of our patrol were through the village and headed toward the beach. I was near the end of the last squad. Then I saw them. Two young men, just standing there. The hair on my neck stood up. They looked out of place. For one thing, they were young men, not children, not women, not old folks. The war had drained this country of all men this age, they were either NVA, VC, ARVN or dead. Secondly, they looked healthy. I could see no signs of leprosy. Finally, they were just staring at me, showing no fear, not even mock subservience. Something was wrong. I immediately peeled off from my squad and walked over to them. They just stood there. I suddenly felt nervous. They looked into my eyes, with no emotion. I asked them, in pidgin Vietnamese, for their identity papers. They hesitated. I raised my rifle, which I was holding in one hand, so that the barrel pointed toward their chests. Their faces changed slightly. They smiled and explained that they didn't have their papers with them. I shifted my feet nervously. We stared at each other. I turned and quickly looked behind me to check on the rest of my squad. A lump formed in my throat as I saw that the squad had kept walking and was now several hundred yards away, not noticing that I had stayed in the village. They were thinking about that turkey dinner. I looked back at the two men. They shrugged their shoulders as if to say, "What now?" I tried to think, but my thoughts were jumbled. I looked again at my squad, drifting further away by the minute. I walked over and quickly checked the men for weapons. They were unarmed and were becoming increasingly polite. I left them standing there and rushed to join my squad. When I turned and looked back into the village, the men were gone.

We reached the beach 15 minutes later. We set in, with the China Sea to our backs, using the dunes as a straight perimeter. Soon the choppers landed and we received large metal containers, inside of which were our promised hot meals. Just as the container for our squad was set down on the top of the dune, automatic fire erupted, 10-12 rounds. The bullets kicked up sand in our faces and tipped our container over, scattering the contents. Turkey and stuffing lay coated with sand. The fire had come from the direction of the village. We sent out a team to investigate, but they found nothing. Later, as I sat eating that crunchy turkey, I thought bitterly of those two men, looking at me and smiling.

Dante's Inferno

11/30/68

Dear Sophia,

Sorry about the stains on the paper, it's the last piece I have. We're low on supplies . . . even water! I don't dream about hamburgers and milkshakes any more, just water, cold, clear water. We've got these pills that make any water fit to drink, but I still get a little queasy when I have to fill my canteen from a mud puddle, Ha! Ha! Anyway, how are you? I hope Jody hasn't been calling on you lately! That's a joke between us marines, but it actually happened to my buddy Cleo. He handled it well though. He's pretty cool. He's from Chicago and he got shot before he joined the Crotch. He was in the Blackstone Rangers, so nothing much fazes him. I better stop talking this way because you won't understand what I'm talking about. I've really changed over here. Thank God I'm short (32 days and a wake up!). I don't want to change so much that I won't be able to change back. But things keep happening. Like a few days ago . . .

Stars and Stripes

"Well, last week, this reporter decided to "tag along" with some marine grunts who were flushing out NVA troops from their temporary base camps west of Khe Sanh. Echo Company was on a three day mini-operation, a thrust across two mountains and down into a valley where what was left of an NVA company was pinned down by two large marine units. Echo Company Captain Eagan reckoned there would be only "the quick and the dead" left by the time his men plugged up the escape route, on day three."

. . . we humped for two days straight, up and then down and on day three, up again. We weren't even sure about what we were doing, but it became clearer as we got about halfway up the second mountain. Somebody was over that ridge. We started to receive sporadic sniper fire and took our first casualties. It was getting hot, too. It must have been 100 degrees. I was carrying the gun (my M-60), lots of rounds over my shoulder and across my chest, my poncho, poncho liner, some C rations and three canteens (two empty and one about ¼ full). Of course we all had flak jackets and helmets. We still had about half a click of climbing ahead of us in order to reach the crest, and then it would be downhill, to meet up with that somebody, probably NVA. We figured it was some kind of mop-up operation, because we had been out for two days with no action until now. Some guys thought we might have missed the action this time and they dreamed of choppers coming to pick us up and carry us back to the firebase. I stopped thinking about it and just focused on putting one foot in front of the other. Suddenly, the terrain changed. We entered a huge area that consisted of large grassy patches as big as several football fields. The patches gradually blended into Elephant Grass, 4-6 feet high and waving back and forth, pushed by a very warm breeze. My throat started to dry up. My stomach tightened and I had this out-of-body feeling that I get sometimes in the bush. I shook it off. I looked left then right and was surprised that I could suddenly see the whole company, spread out across the slope. Strangely, we were still in a jagged line, like a snake, moving up the hill. But almost immediately, the scene faded as the hot wind blew and the grass started to obscure us, slowly, from east to west. Then I was alone, unable to see Nash or Montoya, who were so close to me that I could hear them grunting and swearing. And so it went. We kept marching up that hill, sometimes able to see each other, sometimes totally engulfed by the grass . . .

"As Echo Company swept up the steep plain of the second mountain, they encountered sporadic small arms fire. They responded immediately. In the brief firefight, three marines were wounded. The shooting died down. The flank squads reconnoitered and discovered several blood trails and miscellaneous NVA items such as packs and ammunition belts, indicating a hurried retreat by the enemy. The men moved swiftly up the slope, eager to attack the enemy on the far side of the mountain. Closer to the peak they encountered an estimated 5-10 NVA. They opened fire when the marines were within 200 yards, but the marines, utilizing the Elephant Grass, were able to find cover and slowly advance. The firing was over quickly, as the enemy retreated and disappeared, evidently running up over the top of the hill. The marines suffered two casualties. Again the enemy left few clues as to their actual losses. But it is estimated that they carried several dead and wounded with them in their retreat. Now the marines faced a new foe! The firefight had started a fire on the hillside. The flames spread quickly, feeding on the Elephant Grass, spurred on by the wind."

*. . . Then I heard an AK open up. Damn! It was on our right flank. For a few minutes the rounds were popping, and then it quieted down. I was steadily looking around as I walked, expecting some gunfire from the other side, but it became quiet again. We kept humping up that hill. It was really getting hot now and I started to worry about my lack of water. I was usually good at estimating when we could refill our canteens, but not this time. I walked on. Then we started taking fire from directly in front of us. It seemed more serious, more coordinated than the small firefight on the right flank. I took the 60 off my shoulder and held it by my hip and considered unleashing about 50 rounds. I heard Montoya and Nash open up with their M-16's. We were still in the tall grass. Now I longed for that hot breeze, to blow the sweat out of my eyes. I put the 60 down. I didn't want to give away my position yet. The M-60 fired tracers and the enemy loved to shoot at the machine gunner. I pulled out my 45. I fired three rounds in the direction of the hilltop. My rounds went, "Pop, Pop, Pop." The firing stopped after a few minutes. It was then that I heard screaming. Someone was yelling, "Fire! Fire!" Several marines opened up again, but then it got quiet and suddenly, I smelled smoke. "Oh, **that** kind of fire," I heard Montoya yell. Somehow, the hill had caught fire and the wind was blowing our way. Then the tall grass spread apart and I stumbled into a huge clear area. I looked left and right and watched as the men on each side of me broke through the grass, as I had. I could see for 400 yards to my right and my left. I saw men fall to their knees. Those walking were starting to stagger. My own legs had become like rubber halfway up the hill. I caught a glimpse of Nash's back. He had taken off his flak jacket like he was going to fling it. But he must have changed his mind and was putting it back on. His shirt was black and shiny from the sweat. Montoya looked worse. I walked over to him*

and shared my canteen with him. He gave me a look. I glanced again to my right. The scene had changed. The fire had broken through the tall grass and was moving diagonally up the mountainside. Someone must have dropped some ammo, because rounds starting cooking off. They went, "Crack, crack, crack." I knew it was our stuff from the sound and because the men closest to the noise weren't really ducking. We kept moving. What else could we do? The fire at our backs made us scramble faster. The bad guys in front of us were quiet, but that only made us nervous. They could be anywhere. We were so disoriented from fatigue and edginess that we had ceased to act like anything resembling a unit. Each man just wanted to reach that crest. I thought about the "Killer Teams" we ran out of C-2, just south of Con Thien. No flak jackets, no helmets, just 10 marines, quietly patrolling for three days. We caught a few by surprise that way. That's how to fight this war, I thought, not like this! We kept moving up the hill. Periodically, I would glance across the side of the slope. The shorter, yellow grass shimmered. The smoke formed white puffs which were pushed westward across the troops, by the wind. The sky was bright blue and cloudless. Combined with the smoke and fire it was pretty. We were inching their way up the mountain. We were nearing the crest. Some of the men started to fall, from fatigue or dehydration. A few got up and trudged on but several lay where they fell. I started to panic, but quickly talked myself out of it. I heard numerous cries of, "Corpsman up!" I kept humping. About 20 minutes later, we reached the top. There was a flat area about 100 yards wide and then it started to slope down again. The fire continued to burn across the slope, but luckily, it didn't come over the crest of the mountain. After some confusion, we set up a perimeter. The choppers came to take out the wounded and dead. Rumor had it that 3 marines from 2nd Platoon had died of heat exhaustion. The real casualty figures for Echo Company were, 1 dead, from heat exhaustion, 13 down, temporarily from the heat, 2 men burned by the fire and 6 wounded on the way up the hill. No one was blown away . . .

"The men tried to outrun the fire and stay in their attack formation at the same time. They managed to reach the top of the hill, but several marines suffered burns from the fire. As they readied to attack, word came that the battle below had ended. But the blocking maneuver by Echo Company had been successful in keeping the foe cornered. The final body count was 6 NVA killed and 2 prisoners taken. Hotel Company, 2/1 lost 2 marines KIA and 3 wounded. It is speculated that some NVA managed to escape. The marines of Echo Company, 2/1, in addition to "closing the rear door", captured several maps and battle plans, left by the fleeing NVA scouts. Colonel William Tecumseh Johnson (St. Paul, Minnesota) gave Echo Company a great deal of credit when he said, "The men who climbed that last hill and sealed off the enemy escape route were a big help. They ignored sniper fire and a brush fire that burned right through them, to plug up that gap."

. . . After the choppers left it was quiet for a while. Then we heard that thumping noise again. Sure enough, they were going to pluck us off the top of the hill! First, though, they dropped some water in a huge rubber container, the type they usually drop to troops on long operations. But it bounced and then slid down the mountainside. Then the Hueys came, many of them. I got on one and slid across the floor when the pilot banked. I looked down and there was a green canteen. It looked new. I shook it and realized it was full. I didn't even ask the gunner or anyone else, I just chugged down that water! As we headed back to the firebase, I tried to make sense out of the last three days. But I was a little lightheaded and the chopper was so noisy that I just laid my head back on some ammo boxes and closed my eyes. Like my friend Cleo says, "It ain't nothing but a thing."

Love,
Dave

THE BOOBY TRAP BOYS

We were running patrols out of Cau Ha. When we walked through the leper colony, the villagers eyed us with suspicion and barely concealed hostility. The area was full of tunnels, sand and beaucoup booby traps. The Riviera was a land to fear. Each time a squad or platoon visited Booby Trap Alley, there was a high risk of casualties. We needed a way to neutralize this war of attrition. Captain Eagan devised a plan, which entailed utilizing the skills of the Vietnamese youngsters who often followed us. These kids were mainly orphans and relied on us for food. They loved to wear our gear as well, especially Marine Corps covers. We kept them pretty well fed and occasionally, they would give us hints as to the general location of the VC. They were playing both sides against the middle, but overall, they were just trying to survive. So our CO came up with a good idea. We would pay them to retrieve live booby traps. We gave them MPC, which they converted to Piasters. The kids took to it immediately. I formed a business/friendship relationship with two of them. I met with them every day and they gave me booby traps and I gave them money. Sometimes they would try to scam me by bringing in half of a booby trap one day and the other half the next day. I didn't care. We started to become close. They would hang around, just outside the firebase.

Then they started bringing in a lot of booby traps. Even at the tender age of 18, I suspected that they might be working for the VC. Or maybe they were becoming reckless. One day, my two friends didn't show up. I asked their buddies where they were and they said, "They hurt. They try get VC booby trap. VC Number 10!" I finally located them in a MASH type hospital near Da Nang. They were all bandaged up. One of them had lost a hand. He said, "You number 1 Marine." I turned away so he couldn't see my eyes. The other patients were civilians as well, mainly villagers who had been caught in the middle, wounded by the VC or us. Mostly accidental injuries, the awful collateral damage of war. Or perhaps they had stumbled upon danger, like the booby trap boys. I sat with the boys for a while and then said goodbye. I walked away wondering how much blame I carried. Did I encourage them to become aggressive? Was the booby trap plan a bad idea? I wasn't sure, but I was upset and confused. A few days later, a member of my platoon had his foot blown off by a booby trap. The war continued.

WHORE

"Where will you go with your scarves and your miracles
Who's gonna know who you are
Drugs and wine and flattering light
You must try it again till you get it right
Maybe you'll end up with someone different every night
Your pretty face
It looked so wasted
Another pretty face
Devastated"

Warren Zevon

"Somewhere, somehow, somebody must have
Kicked you around some
Tell me why you wanna lay there,
Revel in your abandon"

Tom Petty

I was always in the bush, or so it seemed. In reality, we had a few days off here and there every month. To relax I mainly smoked pot with the brothers or wrote long letters home. Today I was restless. We were going on patrol in about 12 hours. I had a plan. I weasled my way onto a truck convoy that was headed to Da Nang. When we were just on the outskirts of Da Nang, I jumped off the truck, my flak jacket rattling like wooden shoes from Amsterdam. It was December, 1968. By now, the marines weren't allowed into Dogpatch and they couldn't buy hard liquor at the PX.

No problem. I had a plan. I walked down a dusty dirt road and doubled back in case the MP's were out. I snuck around the corner of a hooch and stepped into a little mini-village. Now I was the only American in sight. I carried my M-16 casually and looked for some orphans. They'd know where to find what I wanted. Sure enough, some kids appeared out of nowhere. "Hey, GI, you want Boom-Boom?" "Hell yes!" They dragged me by my shirt to a little hut. I stepped in and saw a passageway in the back. We slithered through a winding tunnel. They opened a hatch and there she was! She gave me a look. I gulped. She stared right into my eyes. She sat there serenely. I started to sweat. Water popped out of my forehead. I started to take off my pants. My hands were shaking slightly. She kept looking at me. Suddenly there was a noise. Dogs started barking. I heard men yelling. One of the kids said, "You go now!" I said, "NOW? We haven't even started yet!" He rolled his eyes. He grabbed my M-16, which I had propped up against the wall. THAT got my attention! "Gimme that rifle!" I snatched it from his hands. Then I heard Americans talking. It was an MP raid. The kids pushed me into a twelve inch wide space between two walls. I heard shouts and the sound of people running. Then it was quiet. I stuck my head out and she was walking by the doorway. She glanced at me with eyes full of hatred. I didn't get it. What did I do wrong?

ACE

We called him "Ace", the way you might call a short man "Stretch". Among universally young-looking marines, he still stood out. He had the boyish face of a mascot. His build was slight, his arms and chest not defined by bulk or the hardness that comes with sustained labor. He tried his best to fit in with the machine gun crew. He spent two months as an ammo humper, carrying rounds across his chest and over his shoulders. Then by attrition he advanced to assistant machine gunner. He learned to lie next to the gunner; feeding the rounds into the gun and changing the barrel after thousands of rounds were fired in a short period of time. Then one day he became the gunner. He had been in country 6 months. He strutted around the firebase with his .45 pistol prominently displayed. But we could see the fear in his eyes. Some of the men avoided him. He made them feel uneasy. Amid the uncertainty of combat he was at the top of the list to get killed. Nobody came out and said it, but we all saw him as a casualty long before it happened.

One day, several of his buddies visited our firebase. They knew him from back in the states, from Florida. They looked out of place and seemed nervous around us. We had a rough look about us. We carried our weapons at all times, a round in the chamber. They wore fatigues that seemed greener than ours, and their boots . . . their boots were clean and bright. We ignored them. They took Ace aside and spoke to him earnestly. When they left, they were serious and ashen-faced. I was his squad leader. I asked him what they said. He laughed nervously. Then he explained that they had told him to transfer immediately, to get out of the bush. When he had weakly protested, they told him frankly that he would die soon unless he heeded their advice. Then they left. From that day on, Ace became even more skittish. He started to develop reasons to stay behind when we went on patrol. I was in a quandary. Should I make him go, like everyone else? Or should I jeopardize the squad by taking him along, a shaky gunner? I gave in a few times and didn't question his illnesses. But we couldn't keep patrolling shorthanded. I told him I'd support his request for a transfer. But I made it clear I couldn't protect him much longer. Soon he was patrolling with us regularly. Life went on in the bush. I hoped for the best.

Then one day, after 12 months in country, I was pulled from the bush. I became a true "short timer". I relinquished my role as squad leader and prayed that the nightly rocket attacks on our base camp wouldn't result in the irony all short timers feared, and I waited to rotate home, counting the days.

Two weeks before my departure date, a patrol was ambushed, 500 yards outside of our base camp. A platoon rushed out to support them. A daylong firefight ensued. During the course of the day I could sometimes see the fighting, just outside our lines. My short timer status dictated that I had no part to play in this fight. I felt guilty. I couldn't protect Ace anymore. I imagined him firing the machine gun. I knew he'd be a target. I volunteered to take the wounded and killed off the choppers that were bringing men in to the base camp. We were told to separate the wounded so that they could be picked up by another chopper and flown to Da Nang, where they would get triage treatment. Then they would go to a hospital ship, Japan or maybe even back to the states. The KIA would remain at our base camp. When we had time, we would put them into body bags, but utilizing the realism that war demands, our energy was focused on the wounded.

The second chopper I helped unload contained five men. As I pulled one man off, I looked at his face to check his color. It was Ace. He had no apparent wounds. I thought he might be unconscious. He looked like he was sleeping. I checked for wounds, but could find none. Finally I noticed a small entrance wound in his throat. It looked so benign. Then I saw a speck of blood on his lips. I shook him, trying to wake him, trying to help him. I pulled his shirt over his face as the chopper ascended, to shield his eyes from the dust. When the sounds of the chopper receded, I started to carry him to the wounded area. Where was that other chopper, the chopper that would take him to Da Nang?

I struggled to carry him. I saw a marine looking at me, a puzzled look on his face. I shouted to him, demanding that he help me. He pointed over to the KIA area, where two bodies lay. I ignored him, believing he was confused. I looked around. Things seemed strange. I could hear firing in the distance. Someone had taken over the M60, *my old job*, and I could hear the old machine gun roaring. It rattled away, BAM, BAM, BAM, BAM, BAM, BAM ! The battle had moved further away. The wounded were being attended to by a corpsman. Ace lay on the ground. Finally a marine came over and told me that Ace was dead. It seemed like a treacherous thing to say. I gave him a look. I still held out hope that I could save Ace, by willing him alive. I bent down and examined him again. He was still. I looked up again. No one would look at me. Finally the chopper arrived and took the wounded to Da Nang. I walked away in a daze. The fighting finally ended. As our units walked back into the compound, they brought in six prisoners, naked except for shorts and blindfolds. Their hands were tied behind their backs. I looked at them with hatred, but was surprised that my malice was tempered by guilt. Guilt that I hadn't been with my squad this day and guilt that I couldn't stop fate or bad luck or whatever it was that finally took away a young man from Florida, who had no business being in harm's way.

THE VISIT PART I (1968)

Above us loomed the portrait, dominating the small room. It was a den, or maybe a family room. But now it was a shrine, with Gerry's medals prominently displayed. And the giant painting, depicting him in his dress blues, looking somber and formal. My eyes surveyed the scene: his parents huddled together, his sister was weeping, I was staring at the floor.

I had come reluctantly. I knew it would be difficult for everyone. I was only three weeks away from the firefight that had claimed my buddy, my comrade, and their only son. I was home on leave, trying to suppress the dreams. I had debated whether or not to come. I knew they would cry, knew they would ask me for details. I looked up at the wall, at the Purple Heart and Silver Star. But I avoided the painting; I couldn't look into those eyes. Gerry's sister sobbed. The clock ticked. Gerry's parents were staring at me, pleading silently for any information about their sons' last moments. I felt sick. I wished I hadn't come. Finally we talked. I told them the truth. He didn't suffer.

Over the years I visited them, often near the anniversary. The sister never married. The father grew frail. The mother often looked at me strangely, with a gleam of pride. She would remark how well I looked, ask me about my life. She never seemed bitter. Her husband passed away. Her daughter never left home. But the mother prevailed. She visited the monument often. From my home, I would watch her, peering from behind the drapes. After she left, I would walk to the stone, with its flagpole, and pray as well. I often wondered how I happened to buy the home next to the monument. It must be a coincidence, I thought, to now live in Gerry's old neighborhood and to watch over Gerry's mother.

My New Bunker

"Still waking up in the morning with shaking hands. But except in dreams you're never really free. Don't the sun look angry at me."
Warren Zevon

I had planned my mission. Opening the front door was a piece of cake. No problem there. I tapped my pocket and was reassured as the keys jingled. That was the signal to shut the door behind me. I quickly scanned the street. I locked on to the couple across from me, on the opposite sidewalk. They were talking, exchanging gestures with each other. Best to see how this develops, I thought. They finally stopped talking and started drifting away laughing. I glanced around, sweeping the area with an experienced eye. Nothing else seemed amiss, so I started down the walkway, staying in the center. The symmetry of my body, with equal parts of cement on either side pleased me. As I reached the sidewalk I executed a right turn and was on my way. The air was fresh and my breathing was normal. I strode on purposefully. Near the corner, however, I suddenly felt tightness in my throat. There was just no way to see around there. I'd have to take my chances. I considered stepping around and then ducking back, much like a cop would do upon entering a building, but knew that would look foolish. Instead, I held my breath and made the move, my eyes open wide and ears attuned for anything out of the ordinary. I encountered no problems, but up ahead were two groups of people, advancing towards me. Closest to me were two girls, laughing and talking. They weren't paying much attention to anyone but each other. I would easily sidestep them. Behind them were three people: an old man, a younger man and an elderly woman. They were looking straight ahead as they walked, silent and somber. To make matters worse, these groups were close together. I would have to engage them almost simultaneously.

As I started to execute my plan, I also had to check my new flank, the far sidewalk, as well as my rear, since I had moved onto a busier street. A slight throbbing started in my head. The two groups moved closer. The girls were quite noisy, but their words were jumbled, making no sense. The group behind them walked slowly on. I considered crossing the street, but a bus stopped parallel to me, foiling that plan. I surveyed the situation. My gait faltered. I thought I heard steps behind me and whirled my head. When I turned back, they were almost upon me. I knew I had to make a decision. At the last possible moment, I turned and quickly retraced my steps, walking faster so that they wouldn't overtake me. As I neared my home, my breathing became more regular. I hurried up my steps, my keys in hand. As I opened the door, I checked behind me by looking in the glass of the storm door. The coast was clear, no one had followed me. Shutting the door behind me, I felt a combination of embarrassment and relief. I sighed. I promised myself that tomorrow I would go further. I had been back home, in "the world", for a week now.

In College

The silence was deafening. I finally noticed it and gazed out at the sea of faces in the classroom. They were young, well-scrubbed faces. At twenty, I was older than many of the other students. And as a veteran, recently discharged and having spent 13 months in a place that they could only imagine, I had little in common with them.

The assignment was simple enough; put together a demonstration/lecture for a freshman public speaking course. But I was uncomfortable getting up in front of others. Hell, I was uncomfortable everywhere. It was hard readjusting. The other students seemed to have no trouble coming up with topics. One of them brought in a giant toothbrush and demonstrated proper hygiene. Another used a flip chart and discussed evolution. Finally I thought of something! I'd put on a first aid display. I asked for a volunteer and laid the young man on the teacher's desk. "Just lie there. You have a sucking chest wound." I bent over him and explained how to use whatever is at hand. Like a wet tee shirt to cover the wound, and how to stabilize someone until help arrives. As I spoke, I heard the thumping of the medivac chopper in my head. I actually got caught up in the moment, so that any stage fright disappeared. My instincts and practice took over and I was feeling more comfortable by the minute, explaining the steps one should take in a case like this.

Suddenly I heard the silence. I looked up and was first puzzled by the quiet shock on many of their faces. I stopped talking. Then it hit me. This is Quincy College, 1969. Maybe these children are not familiar with such things as sucking chest wounds. I quickly composed myself and finished my presentation. But it was at that moment, in that classroom that I learned to keep my memories private. I vowed to only tell such things to those who belonged to that exclusive club that lets in only combat veterans. I learned at that moment that my memories would be kept in a secret place and only brought out when it was safe.

HERO

The cook was a traitor. He had disgraced himself in the eyes of his family and homeland. This must be true, since Phoi had been told this, repeatedly, at the reeducation camp in Hanoi. He had toiled all day in the sun, with little food or water and then was forced to admit his wrongdoing in the classes at night. "Phoi, how could you leave the National Liberation Front and become a traitor, a friend to the invading Americans?" his interrogator would ask. And after the first year, Phoi could only bow his head and fight back the tears.

Now he worked as a cook, from dawn to dusk. And although he was old, the long hours and constant standing were no problem for him, as he had known much worse. The twelve years in the camp seemed like a dream to him now. He had never suspected that he would one day be released. And of course, he never imagined that he would leave his homeland of Vietnam and travel across the sea to this place, a place he had only heard about, from his friends in Echo Company.

We peered across the rice paddy. The distant tree line was the focus of our gaze. A perfect place for our enemy to hide and wait, and then ambush us. We discussed tactics, talking lowly, while continuously glancing across the dike, behind which we crouched. The squad leader, finally decided to send for the Kit Carson Scout, who was further back, with the Lieutenant. Some of the men were not happy with the decision to get advice from a man who only 6 months ago, was a Viet Cong. Yes, he had been captured and been trained, and then cleared by intelligence to work with the Americans, but most marines were wary and cynical. They suspected that he would revert to form one day, probably at a crucial time. However, they kept their opinions to themselves. They craned their necks and watched as the wiry Kit Carson Scout, who they called Fred, scampered up to their position. He listened to the squad leader and then looked across the rice paddy. Seeming to ignore the tree line, he stared at a low area close by, where two dikes met. He shielded his eyes, squinting at the spot. He took on the appearance of a bird dog, freezing and staring. Finally, he whispered something to the squad leader who blanched slightly. He gathered himself and then nodded. He realigned the squad, so that we faced the area by Fred's design. He gave a hand signal, indicating that they should follow his lead. We were on total alert by now. The squad leader borrowed an M-79 grenade launcher and fired one round, a high graceful arc that dropped in the middle of the area we were scanning. The round exploded with a loud thud. Immediately, six or seven figures rose from the water and grass. They looked like straw men, with weeds and sticks attached to their bodies. They were soaking wet and water rolled off them. The marines cut them down in a hail of bullets. When it was over, Fred had already gone back to the Lieutenant's side. The men had been so concerned about the far tree line that they hadn't seen the enemy who were 50 yards in front of them, lying in wait.

As he cooked, Phoi kept his thoughts to himself. He was a hard worker. However, he didn't mingle with the other employees. While they respected his work ethic, they thought he was strange. He had weird traits. If they came up behind him unannounced, he jumped and shouted at them. He was suspicious. He sometimes cried softly, for no apparent reason.

Over the years, we thought about Fred. We wondered if he made it out on one of those helicopters, near the end of the war. We wondered about his loyalties. Where was his allegiance now? Many of us realized, especially as time went on, that we owed our lives to that former VC.

One day, in 1990, I was having breakfast with an old Marine friend. As usual, we were reminiscing. We talked about that day in the rice paddy. We joked, but our laughter was hollow. We both knew that a skinny, quiet, brave man had saved our lives that day. Just then, we heard a commotion. Through the open door of the kitchen, we glimpsed an old man, an apron around his waist. He was yelling at a waitress. He said, "You no do that! You stay away!" Apparently, she had startled him. We looked at each other and grinned. We knew what it was like to blow up at someone for no reason. We could really identify with him.

COLUMBINE

I sat in my den, transfixed by the snow. Of all the madness, the horror, strangely the snow bothered me the most. As I saw clips of the children running from the high school in Colorado, hands above their heads, I thought back to when I was young, like them. Of course things were different then, I reasoned. There was no comparison. But the more I watched, the closer it seemed. The interviews with survivors. They had that same numbed look. And there was the overall sense of chance. Some lived, some died, at the whim of their enemies or by dumb luck, a few by courage. And the snow continued to fall in the background, white and clean. It confused me. I remembered talking to men with microphones and cameras, at Khe Sanh. Back then, I had that stunned look that the children of Colorado had, the look of guilty survivors. But back then it was hot. It was dry and the dust was red. And the war was in some other country, it was a civil insurgence that we didn't understand. We simply followed orders and crossed off the days on the calendar, hoping that we would someday return to the states. We knew that if we were lucky enough to make it home, we would be safe. We would be back in the land of suburbs and baseball. We could let our guard down. No one would hunt us, no one would shoot at us. But as I saw the children run from the school, those feelings came back. And as I watched the reporters, with the snow falling behind them, I remembered the rounds that rained down on me so many years ago. The screaming rounds that came from the sky. I remembered the feeling of wondering if this was the day I would die. It was a feeling that a youngster shouldn't have to feel, but after a while, it became a part of my life, like the weather. It was clean and crisp, like snow.

SAVING PRIVATE RYAN

I had been visiting the Vet Center for many years. It was like a dance. I would talk about my problems, but when the feelings came up, I'd stop seeing my Counselor for several months. Then I'd come back. I tried to go along with the program. I joined a group that consisted of Vietnam combat vets. I trusted them, but my attendance was spotty. Several of the Counselors were Vietnam combat vets, with Masters Degrees. They were specialists in treating combat veterans who had Post Traumatic Stress Disorder. My Counselor had been treating combat veterans for many years. She sent me to a Veterans Hospital where I was examined by other experts. They told me what I already knew. I had PTSD and was trying to treat myself by drinking alcohol. I finally surrendered after a bad day. While I was watching "Saving Private Ryan", I had a vivid flashback. For a few moments, I was in some sort of battle on a hill in Vietnam. *That did it!*, I said. I went to the Vet Center and asked my Counselor, Tricia, for help. She suggested in-patient treatment at the Coatesville PTSD Unit, at a Veterans Hospital in Pennsylvania. I wearily agreed.

I spent two months in the Unit. There were 40 of us. What a crew! We all had PTSD. We didn't trust each other for a while, but after a few days I felt comfortable with "the boys." I jumped right into the treatment. We learned relaxation techniques, participated in group therapy, individual therapy and writing therapy. We tried Eye Movement Desensitization and Reprocessing Therapy (EMDR), which involves remembering past painful moments. We practiced art therapy. We wrote letters to our comrades who were killed in action in Vietnam. We wrote theoretical letters that were from them to us, which helped us deal with survivor guilt. We learned yoga exercises, which I still do daily. We were told to talk about our experiences in Vietnam, our nightmares, even our fears. This treatment probably saved my life.

I still go to the Vet Center. I still see Tricia. I've traveled by van to Washington, DC with fellow veterans, to pay homage to the monuments. I've hiked up mountains with my comrades, much like we humped in the old days. I'm comfortable at the Vet Center. I drop by some days just to visit. I feel safe there.

VC # 1

He was from North Vietnam. I met him at a tea party at the Joiner Center at the University of Massachusetts, Boston. The Joiner Center studies wars and the social consequences of war. They often host nights like this; some food, a few speeches. We were sipping tea and trying to socialize. He was a poet. I was a writer of true stories that were a part of my recovery program. When I wrote, the words came quickly, tumbling out of my soul. My counselor at the Vet Center, Tricia, had helped me turn my memories into vignettes. He had some poems in his hand. I asked him if I could read them. They had been translated into English in Paris. He said "Yes, you read." I remember his glasses and the fact that he was a full head shorter than me. I read the poems. They were bitter and angry. We were about the same age. I couldn't help but to imagine him shooting at me 40 years ago. He said he had been wounded 6 times. I had to give him credit for that. I had about twenty very close calls in Nam, but I was never wounded. Those around me were far less lucky.

As the H'ors deurves passed by us, he grabbed some rice cakes soaked in sake. He barely spoke a word of English. He finally looked at me and grinned, showing a gold tooth. Then he said, "I love Bill Clinton!" I cracked up and said, "So nice to meet you!" He floated away moving with the current of the room. I saw him talking to some other folks. The next time I looked for him he was gone.

Major Sergeants

"I live in that solitude which is painful in youth, but delicious in the years of maturity."

Albert Einstein

As I entered the International House of Pancakes, I was stunned. There was a large dining area in front of me and a smaller eating area to my right. In the smaller area sat 6 Sgt. Majors! They were by themselves, at one table. They wore khaki shirts and dress blue pants. Their white caps were on the table. Their ribbons indicated Middle East service, with good conduct and combat. I thought back to the days of Platoon 3020 at Parris Island, Advanced Infantry Training at Camp Lejeune, Jungle Warfare School, Okinawa and Vietnam. I had never seen more than one Sgt. Major at a time! Additionally, these men were young! I finally realized that they were recruiters, like Sgt. Shaunessy, the Marine who had signed me up. My dad had to come with me to the recruiting station, to co-sign the enlistment papers, as I was 17 ½ years old.

When I was in the Marine Corps, I thought that Sgt. Majors were ancient! They were crusty and profane. These Marines looked fairly wholesome. I wondered, "Is rank quicker now?" I hesitated, then walked past the waitress, into the private dining area.

The Sgt. Majors eyed me suspiciously. I walked to their table. They all stopped eating. I gave them a look. I said, "My, my! A flock of Sgt. Majors!" They said nothing. All eyes were on me. I enjoyed the confusion and even their rising hostility. I waited a beat and said, "Grunt, 1968, Vietnam." They paused for a second and then they all started smiling. They said, almost in unison, "Semper Fi!" I know the code words. I nodded and left, feeling an overwhelming sense of pride. I also felt a weird sense of sorrow, perhaps thinking of my buddies from Con Thien. Perhaps not . . .

COWARD

Strangely, _____ was not afraid during the fire fights and incoming. But in those interim periods, when there was down time, the fear would become all encompassing. He would think about the days before all of this, when he was safe and when things were easy. Then he would think of various ways to get out of this mess. He could put peanut butter on his bare toe and hope that a rat would bite him during the night, but the thought of those painful rabies shots nixed that idea. He could shoot himself through the palm, but then there would be telltale powder burns. Finally he came up with a good idea. The next time the rounds came in, as he huddled in the trench, he thrust his arm up, waving it as if to attract the shrapnel. The first two times it didn't work. But then, one afternoon, as he raised his arm, almost as if to say, "Call on me teacher, I know the answer!", it happened. He felt a searing pain and when he lowered his arm and looked at his hand, sure enough, it was covered in blood. He had caught several pieces of hot metal, just like he used to catch fire flies back home. It was his trigger hand, and he lost the feeling in the entire hand (he swore). He was sent first to Da Nang, then to the hospital ship, then to Japan, and finally back to the states. They changed his MOS and he spent the rest of the war working as a driver in the motor pool at Quantico, Virginia. He hardly ever thought of the patrols, the bunkers or his comrades, who had sent him off with a cheerful ribbing about his "million dollar wound". Occasionally, he wondered what they would say if they knew the full story. But when that thought entered his mind he pushed it away.

Now it is forty years later. _____ sits patiently in his car as the traffic comes to a complete stop on the highway. In the car behind him, a family also waits for the traffic to start moving again. One young boy looks at the car in front and says to his father, "Dad, why does that man have a funny license plate?" The father looks at the plate and replies, "That's a Purple Heart license plate. That man was wounded in combat. I guess you could say he's a hero."

THE VISIT PART II (2008)

I still own the house next to Gerry's monument. I keep the monument clean and beautiful. Every spring I place 16 small American flags along the walkway to the monument. I make sure that a big, clean flag flies on the flagpole. My Marine Corps buddies help me sweep, rake and cut the grass. We wash the granite stone with water. People stop at the monument for many reasons. They read the inscription on the stone and they read the poem. The neighborhood kids are very respectful. Sometimes, a couple of his high school friends visit the monument. They went to college when Gerry joined the Marine Corps. I watch them from behind my curtains, wondering who they are.

Every evening I walk my neighbor's dog. We often pass by the home where Gerry lived, before the fighting, before the war. I have stopped by several times over the years to say hello to his mother and sister. His father died years ago. His sister never married. She lived at home with her mother. The last time I saw his mother, she had trouble hearing me, so I stooped down and told her that her son was a wonderful man, very brave. She smiled. The next time I went by the house it looked different; the drapes were new, the mailbox was new, etc. I rang the doorbell and a Vietnamese man appeared. He told me that Gerry's mother had moved to a retirement community in Arizona. I felt as if part of my mission was accomplished. But when I returned to my street, I immediately realized that the shrubs near the monument needed to be trimmed. The flowers needed watering. There was still work to be done.

Poems

I Saw Chesty at the Mall

(This poem is dedicated to all of our Marine Corps brothers who served during the Korean War)

"He, who would pass his declining years with honor and comfort, should, when young, consider that he may one day become old, and remember when he is old, that he has once been young."
Joseph Addison

"All right, they're on our left, they're on our right, they're in front of us, they're behind us . . . they can't get away this time."
Chesty Puller

Yea, I walk through the valley of the mall with an uneasy step.
So many sounds, so many flashes.
The toy stores are like ammo dumps, the T shirts are brown or green; familiar colors.
The pants have many pockets, perhaps to hide *pistolas*, maybe to conceal C 4 fuses.
Doc Marten boots clomp on the hard, shiny tiles. The army of the young marches on.
I hear that old helicopter noise, look around and see only the shiny faces of cell phone people.
Then, I see an older man, he of the Frozen Chosen, sitting on an uncomfortable bench,

Near two vixens with visible thongs. They ignore him.

He sips a black coffee and looks on, with that old thousand-yard stare.

He's remembering a time when heaven was warm and safe; hell was upon him.

His wife's pocketbook sits between his legs. He guards it, much as he guarded his ammo,

Back in the days when Truman strolled through the streets of America.

His jacket caresses his large, but frail body.

Inside his pocket are two blurry pictures of a boy who was told to "fix bayonets" one day,

On a hill nobody remembers.

He's grateful to be alive. He lives for the days when his granddaughter climbs onto his sore knees.

Today at the mall, he smiles as the children race past him, on winged sneakers.

I continue my march. Eventually, I tire. I sit and think of elephant grass waving in the sun.

The children rush by me, smiling, talking, not seeing me.

My cap and my jacket they comfort me.

GERRY

(This poem is dedicated to Gerald Bradley, my friend and comrade)

We met over there, in a land 10,000 miles from Braintree.
We were young warriors, Marines with clear eyes and brave hearts.
You, broad shouldered from lifting weights and playing hockey.
Me, rail thin and still boyishly awkward.

Together, we fought terrifying battles.
In the mountains, from foxholes quickly dug, while the rounds descended
    upon us.
In rivers and in mud, chest high.
In rice paddies, as the rain pounded as hard as our hearts.

We never ran away from our fear, much as many of us wished we could.
You were different though.
Didn't you dread the withering fire?
Were you born brave?
Your leadership and crisp orders gave us hope and guidance.
We thought you were invincible.

Then, one day, in that terrible area we called "The Riviera", you fell.
It happened as you were leading your men, as usual;
Standing, firing, while some hugged the ground with sweat-drenched
    bodies.
Our noble enemy always targeted the leaders, the bravest fighters.

For your bravery, your country bestowed the Silver Star upon you.
But this monument stands as a symbol of our respect.
You are a true hero, Gerry.
You will never be forgotten.
And we know that you don't sleep here;
But instead continue to stand watch, so that we may rest, safe and secure.

Semper Fidelis!

THE OLD WARRIOR

Sitting in his den, the man sighs.
He takes the album from the shelf.
He looks at the pictures, remembers and cries.

Old black and white memories.

Pictures of him, was he ever that lean?
His face fresh and eager.
He and his friends, trying to look mean.

They were out in the bush, looking for action,
In jungles, rice paddies and in the highlands.
But inside they were scared, a normal reaction.

Scared that their time might come too soon.

Not that they'd tell you, not then, anyway.
They kept their fear to themselves.
But as the years pass, the bravado slips away.

He counts the men in the last picture, the number was five.
They were young and brave.
Three made it home, glad to be alive.
Now the photos are yellow, the uniform packed away,
Some of the names are long forgotten.

But the memories become clearer, stronger each day.
He closes his eyes and can feel the heat,
Feels the lump in his throat,
Hears the choppers they ran to meet.

As the rounds zipped past him.

He remembers the ponchos they loaded aboard.
They were as heavy as his heart,
Since inside them were his friends, going home to the Lord.

Years later, the man asks God, "Why?
For what reason did those young men die?"
Today, he knows there is no clean answer
To such questions as these.
Why is there killing, why is there cancer?
He only knows that he lived to return,
Came home with relief,
While others died, but what lesson was learned?
Perhaps their sacrifice saved others who saw the madness,
Saw the names on the wall
And stopped short of war, remembering their sadness.

But history tells us war will come again,
Requesting our sons, the pride of our country.
And on that day may we send the best men.
Men who will fight for a noble goal,
Men fully trained who will fulfill their mission,
And may come home quickly, healthy and whole.

Men who will look at their pictures and cry,
Remember their friends, remember the fear,
But know they were right and not wonder why.

He closes the book, careful not to bend the photos
He tries to quiet the noises, still the memories
He looks at the picture on the wall, of his family
And tries not to feel guilty for coming home alive.

Terminology

1) Short-Timer = A Marine who only has about 2 weeks or so until he rotates home to the US.
2) KIA = Killed in action.
3) WIA = Wounded in action.
4) VC = Viet Cong.
5) NVA = North Vietnamese Army soldier.
6) AK 47 = Chinese assault rifle.
7) Sky Pilot, Padre = Chaplain, minister, rabbi or priest.
8) Frag or Fragging = The act of killing or trying to kill an officer.
9) Dear John Letter = A letter from a girlfriend in America that said she wasn't going to wait for her Marine boyfriend to come home. She was going to get a new boyfriend.
10) Jody = The name we gave to any guy back in America who stole a Marine's girlfriend while the Marine was in Vietnam.
11) Grunt = Infantryman. The men who did the actual fighting (approximately 15% of the soldiers in Vietnam were grunts; the rest were truck drivers, cooks, electricians, intelligence analyzers, construction workers, etc.)
12) Booby Trap = Hidden explosive devices that were planted on trails where Marines would patrol. If a booby trap was stepped on, it could mean the loss of a foot, or even the death of 5 or 6 Marines.
13) LZ = Landing zone for a helicopter.
14) C Rations = Canned food that the "grunts" ate.
15) 45 = 45 caliber pistol.
16) M 16 = Rifle carried by the Marines.
17) M 60 = Machine gun carried by a few marines (this is what I carried).

18) Hump = Walk
19) Clicks = Kilometers
20) Saddle Up = Put on protective vests (flak jackets), helmets, fill canteens with water, strap on as much ammunition as possible and get ready to go on patrol.
21) Tet Offensive, 1968 = Tet is the Vietnamese New Year. In 1968 all hell broke loose and the Americans were attacked in dozens of key cities, outposts and hills. The Americans killed 50,000 enemy, but the shock of the attacks fueled the antiwar movement back in the USA.
22) The Crotch = The Marine Corps
23) The Blackstone Rangers = A black street gang from Chicago. Many BSR joined the Marine Corps.
24) "Stars and Stripes" = The official newspaper of the USA in Vietnam. We barely read it, because it was too one-sided; "America is great, we can do no wrong," etc.
25) "It ain't nothing but a thing." = A saying that really meant, "This is bad, but we don't have time to grieve or get depressed."
26) Phantom = Jet. These jets often flew very close to the ground and dropped napalm (liquid fire) and bombs on the enemy.
27) Kit Carson Scout = A VC who had been captured by Marines, screened by the Intelligence Division, and had agreed to go on patrols with the Marines, to help them locate booby traps, hidden ammunition, tunnels and the enemy. Some were very helpful, but we never fully trusted them.
28) MOS = Numerical job description (grunt was 0311, machine gunner was 0330).
29) Purple Heart = Award given to any combatant injured in the line of duty.
30) "The World" = USA.
31) ARVN = Army of the Republic of Vietnam. Vietnamese military allies of the Marines. Our other allies in Vietnam were South Koreans (ROKS) and Australians.
32) The Bush = The jungle or hills or rice paddies. Any place where a few (6-30) Marines were "on their own" Any dangerous place.
33) Hooch = House.